D0483530

THE
TOTALLY
CHILE PEPPER
COOKBOOK

Text copyright © 1994 by Helene Siegel and Karen Gillingham.
Illustrations copyright © 1994 by Ani Rucki. All rights reserved.
No part of this book may be reproduced or transmitted in any form
or by any means, electronic or mechanical, including photocopying,
recording, or by any information storage and retrieval system
without permission in writing from the publisher.

Printed in Singapore

The Totally Chile Pepper Cookbook is produced by becker&mayer!, Ltd.

Cover illustration and design: Dick Witt

Interior design and typesetting: Dona McAdam, Mac on the Hill

Library of Congress Cataloging-in-Publication Data:
Siegel, Helene.
        The totally chile pepper cookbook / by Helene Siegel & Karen
Gillingham.
            p. cm.
        ISBN 0-89087-724-6 ; $4.95
        1. Cookery (Hot peppers) 2. Hot peppers   I. Gillingham, Karen.
II. Title.
TX803.P46554 1994
641.6 ' 384—dc20   94-1224
                                                                CIP

Celestial Arts
PO Box 7123
Berkeley, CA 94707

Other cookbooks in this series:
The Totally Garlic Cookbook
The Totally Mushroom Cookbook
The Totally Corn Cookbook

THE
TOTALLY
CHILE PEPPER
COOKBOOK

by Helene Siegel and Karen Gillingham
Illustrations by Ani Rucki

CELESTIAL ARTS
BERKELEY, CA

CONTENTS

L ike many Americans who came to chile peppers late in life, we approached them cautiously. Nobody said an ingredient that caught us in the back of the throat and throttled us, brought tears streaming from our eyes, made our hearts palpitate and lips tingle was going to be easy to love.

But then chile peppers snuck up on us and struck some elemental flavor chords. In neighborhood joints we ate fabulous chiles rellenos made of fresh-roasted poblanos—rather than wimpy canned Anaheims—that surprised us with their depth of flavor. Fiery, fruity, smokey salsas gave sparkle to ordinary grilled meats, poultry, and fish. While the spicy foods from Szechuan had reawakened our tired taste buds years ago, when we tasted the sophisticated sweet, sour, spicy, and salty harmony that is Thai food we felt we were on to something more than mere infatuation. Call it chile love.

In the new low-fat, low-salt, little-meat American kitchen, the name of the game is flavor. And as this continent's natives have always known, chiles have it.

Along with their legendary heat, they add a jolt of clear, bright, stimulating flavor.

Peppers range from brightly spicy little serranos and Thais to mysteriously smokey chipotles and dried fruit-flavored anchos. They can add an element of greater complexity to anything you cook, literally from soup to nuts, and they can be used as subtly or aggressively as any other spice once you understand how to cook with them.

A good place to begin is by experimenting with a few easy-to-find chiles like jalapeños or anchos and taste for yourself what happens when the seeds are left in or omitted from a dish. Next, see what happens when the pepper is roasted and seeded. Now you are beginning to see the chile's depth of character.

All of the quantities, scales of heat (from one to three, indicated by little chile symbols, of course), and seeding instructions supplied in the following recipes are purely subjective. Use as little or as much chile as you wish and add the seeds according to desire. Your taste buds will thank you for it.

CONTENTS

FIERY
ADDITIONS

CHILE OIL

¾ cup peanut oil
¼ cup dark sesame oil
1½ tablespoons dried red chile flakes
Several whole dried red chiles

In small saucepan, combine oils and set over medium heat for 3 minutes. Add chile flakes and immediately remove from heat. Cover and let stand overnight. Strain through fine sieve into clean bottle, discarding flakes. Drop a few whole dried chiles into oil for decoration and seal. Store in cool place.

Makes 1 cup.

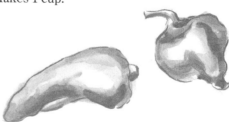

THAI VINAIGRETTE

4 serranos or green Thais, stemmed
2 garlic cloves, chopped
1 teaspoon minced ginger
1 tablespoon Thai fish or soy sauce
3 tablespoons lime juice
1/4 cup peanut oil

Combine all ingredients in a blender and purée until smooth.

Makes about 1/2 cup.

FRESH RED CURRY PASTE

6 red jalapeños, stemmed, seeded, and
   coarsely chopped
4 stalks lemongrass, trimmed and thinly sliced
1/4 cup coarsely chopped shallots
2 tablespoons cilantro leaves
1 tablespoon coarsely chopped garlic
1 tablespoon chopped fresh ginger
1 tablespoon Thai fish sauce
1 tablespoon peanut oil
2 teaspoons ground coriander
1 teaspoon freshly grated lime rind
1/2 teaspoon ground cumin
11/2 teaspoons salt
1/2 teaspoon black pepper

In food processor, combine all ingredients.
Process until paste forms. Use on fish to be
steamed, to infuse oil for stir-frys, or as sauce
or salsa for grilled meats and fish.

Makes about 3/4 cup.

RED JALAPEÑO JELLY

- 8 red jalapeños, stemmed, seeded, and coarsely chopped
- 3 red bells, stemmed, seeded, and coarsely chopped
- 6 cups sugar
- 1½ cups vinegar
- 1 (6-ounce) bottle liquid pectin
  Red food coloring (optional)

In food processor, combine jalapeños and bells. Process until puréed. Transfer to large saucepan along with sugar and vinegar. Bring to boil and cook 1 minute. Remove from heat and let stand 5 minutes. Stir in pectin. If desired, add few drops red food coloring. Mix well. Strain into hot sterilized jars and seal.

Makes 3 pints.

CONTENTS

INCENDIARY
SOUPS, SALADS
& SAVORY BITES

TORTILLA PASILLA SOUP

Long, thin, dried chiles pasillas are the traditional condiment in tortilla soup.

6 dried pasillas
12 corn tortillas
1 small onion, chopped
2 garlic cloves, chopped
1 (28-ounce) can chopped tomatoes
Oil for frying
1 quart chicken broth
1/4 cup chopped cilantro
Coarse salt and freshly ground pepper
1 avocado, peeled and sliced
1 cup crumbled panela or feta cheese
Additional chopped cilantro

In dry skillet, toast pasillas over medium-high heat, turning frequently, for 3 minutes. When cool enough to handle, remove stems, break open, remove seeds, and crumble pasillas. Place about a third of pasillas in small bowl and set aside. Reserve remaining pasillas.

In same skillet, heat about ¾ inch oil. Add tortilla strips in several batches and fry until crisp and golden. Drain on paper towels. Pour off all but about 2 tablespoons oil.

In food processor, combine reserved pasillas, onion, garlic, and tomatoes with liquid. Add blended mixture to reserved oil in skillet and cook over medium-high heat 3 to 4 minutes. Transfer mixture to large saucepan. Add broth and bring to boil. Simmer 20 minutes. Stir in cilantro. Season to taste with salt and pepper.

To serve, place handful of tortilla strips in each of 6 soup bowls. Pour hot soup over tortillas. Pass remaining pasillas, avocado, and cheese at table to be added as desired.

Serves 6.

POTATO POBLANO SOUP

When combined with soothing potatoes and milk, roasted poblanos create a subtle undercurrent of pepper power.

4 tablespoons butter
3 garlic cloves, chopped
1 medium onion, chopped
2 poblanos, roasted, peeled, seeded, and chopped
1 teaspoon ground cumin
Salt and black pepper
4 cups chicken stock
2 pounds boiling potatoes, chopped with skins
1 cup milk

Melt butter in large stockpot over medium-high heat. Sauté garlic, onions, poblanos, cumin, salt, and pepper until onions are soft, about 7 minutes.

Add chicken stock and potatoes. Bring to boil, reduce to simmer, and cook, uncovered, until potatoes are tender, 30 minutes. Transfer to food processor or blender and purée until smooth.

Return to stockpot, add milk, and bring back to a boil. Serve hot.

Serves 4.

Poblanos are a medium-sized, thick-skinned, triangular-shaped dark-green chile with full-bodied chile flavor as well as good heat. It is a favorite for roasting and stuffing (chiles rellenos don't get much better than those made with these). The good news is they are starting to show up with some regularity at the supermarket.

THAI SHRIMP SOUP

12 ounces medium shrimp
1 tablespoon vegetable oil
 Salt
2 Thai green chiles, seeded and slivered
 Grated zest of 2 limes
2 stalks lemongrass, cut in 2-inch lengths
4 cups chicken stock
 Juice of 2 limes
2 teaspoons Thai fish sauce
1/2 bunch chopped cilantro, 3 sliced scallions, and 1 red Thai chile, seeded and diced for garnish

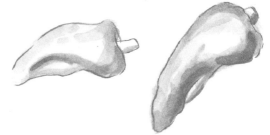

Peel and devein shrimp, reserving shells.

In heavy pot, heat oil over high heat. Sauté shells with salt until pink, about a minute. Add serranos, lime, and lemongrass and sauté less than a minute.

Pour in chicken stock, bring to boil, and simmer 20 minutes. Strain, discarding solids, and pour broth back into pot. Bring to low boil. Add shrimp, lime juice, and fish sauce and simmer until shrimp are done, about 2 minutes. Sprinkle in cilantro, scallions, and red chiles and serve hot.

Serves 4.

PEPPER'S PLEASURE PAIN PRINCIPLE

Here is how it works: When capsaicin (the chemical that carries the heat) touches the nerves on the tongue and mouth, it sends the message: "Help! There is a fire in here and I think we are going to die!" to the brain. The brain responds by trying to put out the fire. It sends the mucous system into overdrive, makes the heart beat faster, produces quantities of sweat, and finally releases endorphins, the body's natural painkiller. The so-called chile high is the feeling you get when endorphins are running around your body but the fire has already gone out.

COLD CHINESE NOODLES WITH SPICY PEANUT SAUCE

Pepper has traditionally been a staple of peasant diets in southern Third-world countries—where bland starches like rice, beans, and tortillas benefit from chile's sparkle. Modern field workers in Mexico's Yucatan peninsula have been seen making a meal of roasted habanero tacos.

1/2 pound dry Chinese egg noodles
    or spaghettini
    Sesame oil

Sauce:

  2 garlic cloves
    1/4-inch length fresh ginger
  2 tablespoons soy sauce
1/4 cup smooth peanut butter
  1 tablespoon sesame oil
  2 tablespoons water
  1 tablespoon chili oil
  1 tablespoon brown sugar
  2 peeled and shredded cucumbers,
    1/4 cup chopped fresh cilantro, and
    red pepper flakes for garnish

Bring a large stockpot of salted water to a boil. Cook the noodles until al dente. Drain, rinse with cold water, and transfer to bowl. Toss with a spoonful or two of sesame oil and set aside at room temperature.

Mince garlic and ginger in food processor or blender. Add remaining ingredients, except garnish, and purée until smooth. Pour over noodles and toss well. Sprinkle with cucumber, cilantro, and red pepper flakes. Serve at room temperature.

Serves 4.

India produces the largest chile crop worldwide. Other big producers are China, Pakistan, Mexico, Sri Lanka, Nigeria, Ethiopia, Thailand, and Japan. The state of Texas, practically a country, is presently pursuing jalapeño farming, since farmers have learned it is second in profitability only to marijuana.

23

CRISP STUFFED JALAPEÑOS

In 1937 the Nobel prize was awarded to Hungarian scientist Albert Szent-Györgyi for his discovery that chiles are a rich source of vitamin C. They also are high in vitamins A and E, potassium, and folic acid and are incomparable for clearing sinuses and cleansing pores.

Capsaicin, in the chemical form of guafenesin, is a key ingredient in commercial expectorants like Vicks 44, Sudafed, and Robitussin.

3/4 cup vinegar
  Salt
12 medium jalapeños
12 small cooked shrimp
  or 12 whole blanched
  almonds
1/2 cup or more shredded
  jack or panela cheese
  All-purpose flour
 3 eggs, separated
  Freshly ground pepper
  Oil for frying

With sharp knife, make slit along one side of each jalapeño, leaving stems intact. Remove seeds, if desired. Stuff each with 1 shrimp or almond and some cheese or entirely with cheese. Coat with flour.

Beat egg whites with mixer until soft peaks form. In separate bowl, beat egg yolks lightly with 1 tablespoon flour and salt and pepper to taste. Gently fold into whites. Pour oil into heavy deep skillet to depth of 1 inch. Heat to 375 degrees F.

Holding each prepared jalapeño by stem, dip into batter to coat. Drop into hot oil and fry, turning once, until golden. Drain on paper towels. Serve hot.

Serves 4 to 6.

The jalapeño, America's favorite chile, is a thick-fleshed, small (about 3 inches long), bright-green hot pepper that shows up in just about everything these days from corn muffins to vodka. In Mexico, where most of ours come from, they are eaten out of hand as a snack food. Jalapeños are milder than serranos and make a great raw garnish for soups, salsas, and stews. The red variety is milder and sweeter. Also sold pickled and canned.

PEPPERED GARBANZOS

Oil for deep frying
1 (15-ounce) can garbanzo beans, drained
1 tablespoon chopped cilantro or parsley
Dried pequins, stemmed and crumbled
Coarse salt and freshly ground pepper

In wok or deep skillet, heat about 1 inch oil to 375 degrees F.

Rinse beans and pat dry with paper towels. Fry, in two batches, just until crisp, about 30 seconds. Remove with slotted spoon and drain on paper towels. Transfer to bowl and sprinkle with cilantro, crumbled pequins, and salt and pepper to taste. Serve immediately.

Serves 4.

HELLBENT ALMONDS

We can't imagine a better way to wash down a frosty margarita.

> 2 tablespoons Chile Oil (see p. 10)
> 2 to 3 dried pequins, stemmed and crumbled
> 1/2 teaspoon ground cumin
> 1 teaspoon sugar
> 2 cups blanched whole almonds
> Coarse salt

Preheat oven to 300 degrees F. In skillet, heat oil. Add pequins, cumin, and sugar and cook, stirring, 1 to 2 minutes. Add almonds and mix to coat evenly. Spread almonds on baking sheet and bake 15 minutes, stirring occasionally. Sprinkle with salt to taste. Serve cool.

Makes 2 cups.

QUESO FUNDIDO WITH CHIPOTLES

1 pound jack cheese, shredded
1 cup crumbled cotija or feta cheese
3 to 4 canned chipotles in adobo sauce
1 small red bell pepper
1 bunch green onions, trimmed
2 to 3 tablespoons chopped fresh cilantro
12 hot corn or flour tortillas
   Salsa Fresca (see p. 68)
   Guacamole (optional)

Preheat oven to 300 degrees F.

In lightly oiled 9-inch square baking dish or shallow casserole, scatter cheeses in even layer. Cut chipotles into strips and scatter over cheese. Bake until melted and bubbly around edges, about 15 minutes.

Meanwhile, grill red bell over hot coals or run under hot broiler, turning, until blackened on all sides. Peel, stem, seed, and cut into strips. Grill or broil green onions just until limp.

Sprinkle melted cheese with cilantro and spoon onto hot tortillas with grilled pepper strips and onions. Top with Salsa Fresca and guacamole, if desired.

Serves 6.

Chipotles or dried, smoked red jalapeños add a special sweet, smokey dimension to the foods they are matched with. If dried chiles are hard to find, substitute chipotles canned in adobo (a sweet and spicy barbecue sauce) or moritas, a dried, smoked jalapeño. But be careful. These little honeys can be habit forming.

THAI MELON SALAD

6 cups melon cubes, such as honeydew,
  cantaloupe, or crenshaw
2 cucumbers, halved lengthwise and sliced
6 tablespoons lime juice
¼ cup honey
  Grated zest of 1 lime
¼ teaspoon salt
1 red Thai chile, diced with seeds
2 tablespoons chopped fresh cilantro

Combine melon and cucumber in salad bowl.

Mix remaining ingredients together in small bowl. Pour over fruit, toss well, and serve or chill up to 2 hours. This gets hotter as it sits.

Serves 4.

POBLANO CORN QUESADILLAS

These simple quesadillas owe their terrific flavor to the earthy combination of corn tortillas and roasted poblanos.

Vegetable oil for coating
4 corn tortillas
2 cups grated Monterey jack, panela and/or
   cotija cheese
1 large poblano, roasted, seeded, peeled, and
   cut in strips
Chopped tomatoes and onion for garnish.

Preheat oven to 200 degrees F.

Lightly coat medium cast-iron skillet with oil and place over medium-low heat. Heat tortillas, two at a time, a few seconds just to heat, and then flip over. Sprinkle with cheeses to within 1/2 inch of edge and scatter with chile strips. Fold over with spatula and press to enclose. Cook, turning frequently, until cheese begins to ooze, about 3 minutes. Keep quesadillas warm in oven while completing remainder. Cut into wedges and serve with tomatoes and onion.

Serves 4.

SPICY JAPANESE SLAW

1 Napa cabbage, trimmed and shredded
3 green onions, trimmed and thinly sliced
1/2 cup chopped cilantro
3 red jalapeños, stemmed, seeded, and minced
1 (3-ounce) package Oriental-flavor ramen noodle soup mix
1/2 cup vegetable oil
2 teaspoons sesame oil
1/4 cup rice vinegar
1/2 teaspoon sugar
1 tablespoon sesame seeds, toasted
Coarse salt and freshly ground pepper

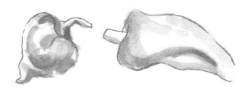

In large bowl, combine cabbage, green onions, cilantro, and jalapeños. Remove noodles from soup mix and break into small bite-sized pieces. Add to cabbage mixture.

In small bowl, whisk oils with vinegar, sugar, and contents of seasoning packet from soup mix. Pour over salad and toss thoroughly. Add sesame seeds and salt and pepper to taste. Toss to mix.

Serves 4 to 6.

HOW THE CHILE GOT ITS NAME

One of the great new foods that Columbus found on his seriously bungled quest for spices and a shortcut to India back in 1492 was aji, or chile. In Europe, it was renamed Calcutta pepper by German botanist Leonard Fuchs, who believed (along with everyone else) that Columbus had found India. The original word for chile peppers in Nahuatl, the Mexican Indian language, is chilli.

ORANGES & JICAMA WITH PEQUIN VINAIGRETTE

8 oranges, peeled and sectioned, white pith removed
2 cups peeled, chopped jicama
1 bunch watercress, torn into pieces
1/2 red onion, thinly sliced
1/4 cup vegetable oil
2 tablespoons lime juice
1 to 2 dried pequins, stemmed and crushed
Coarse salt and freshly ground pepper

In large bowl, combine oranges, jicama, watercress, and onion.

In blender, combine oil, lime juice, and pequins. Blend until pequins are finely ground. Season to taste with salt and pepper. Pour over salad and toss thoroughly.

Serves 6 to 8.

THAI BEEF SALAD

1 pound boneless rib eye steak
1/2 cup soy sauce
1 teaspoon sesame oil
4 teaspoons sugar
3 jalapeños, stemmed, seeded, and minced
1/4 cup peanut oil
1/4 cup lime juice
2 tablespoons Thai fish sauce
1/4 cup coarsely chopped unsalted dry-roasted
   peanuts
1/4 cup sliced green onion
1/4 cup chopped cilantro
6 cups thinly sliced Romaine or Napa cabbage
   Tomato wedges, cucumber slices, carrot curls

Place steak in shallow dish. Combine ¼ cup soy sauce, sesame oil, and 1 teaspoon sugar. Pour over steak. Marinate at least 1 hour, turning several times.

Meanwhile, in blender, combine remaining soy sauce and sugar, jalapeños, peanut oil, lime juice, fish sauce, peanuts, green onion, and cilantro. Process until nuts are finely chopped.

Grill steak over hot coals, turning once, until done as desired. Let stand 5 minutes. Slice steak thinly on diagonal and place in bowl. Pour half of dressing over meat and toss to coat.

On each of 4 individual plates, divide and arrange lettuce. Arrange meat, tomato, cucumber, and carrots on each plate. Pass additional dressing at table.

Serves 4.

CONTENTS

OVER-THE-TOP ENTRÉES

SALMON WITH CITRUS HABANERO SALSA

This easy but impressive dish of salmon would be great served on a bed of thinly sliced cucumbers doused with rice vinegar and a side of rice to offset the heat.

4 tomatoes, roughly chopped
4 tomatillos, husked and chopped
1/2 onion, peeled and roughly chopped
1 to 2 habaneros, seeded and chopped
1 tablespoon olive oil
1/2 teaspoon salt
1/2 teaspoon ground cumin
1/4 teaspoon cinnamon
   Juice of 3 oranges
4 (6-ounce) salmon fillets
4 tablespoons butter

Combine tomatoes, tomatillos, onion, and habanero in blender and purée until smooth.

Heat oil in medium sauce-pan over high heat. Pour in purée, salt, cumin, and cinna-mon and boil about 7 minutes. Skim and discard foam from top. Pour in orange juice, reduce heat, stir, and cook 1 minute longer. Strain, if desired, return to pan and beat in 2 tablespoons butter till smooth. (Butter can be omitted.)

Season fish all over with salt and pepper. Melt 2 tablespoons butter in skillet over high heat. Sear fish 2 minutes per side, then reduce heat and cook 2 minutes more per side. Serve topped with sauce.

Serves 4.

The powerful little habanero from Mexico's Yucatan has such a devoted following it is now available dried in supermarkets. You still may have to haunt farmer's or specialty markets for the fresh variety, which has better flavor. This little orange lantern-shaped, walnut-sized chile is rated, along with the Scotch Bonnet from the Caribbean, the world's hottest chile. We like to remove the seeds and purée it to make sauces for fish. A little goes a long way!

ANCHO SEAFOOD CHILI

8 dried anchos
1 onion, diced
2 tablespoons vegetable oil
3 garlic cloves, minced
1 (28-ounce) can chopped tomatoes
1 (18-ounce) can tomatillos, drained and cut up
1 cup dry white wine
2 teaspoons dried crumbled oregano
1 teaspoon ground cumin
1/2 teaspoon ground coriander
1 bay leaf
1/2 pound each large shelled shrimp, bay
    scallops, and squid rings, uncooked
12 each small clams and mussels, uncooked
    Coarse salt and freshly ground pepper
    Chopped cilantro and jalapeños, crumbled
    cotija or feta cheese, and lime wedges

In saucepan, cover anchos with water. Bring
to boil. Remove from heat, cover, and let stand
10 minutes.

Meanwhile, in large pot, sauté onion in oil
until soft. Add garlic and cook 30 seconds longer.
Stir in tomatoes, tomatillos, wine, oregano,
cumin, coriander, and bay leaf. Bring to boil
then reduce heat and simmer 15 minutes.

Meanwhile, drain, peel, stem, and seed
anchos. Place in blender with 1/2 cup tomato
mixture from pan and process until puréed.
Stir into tomato mixture and simmer 15 minutes
longer.

Stir shrimp, scallops, and squid into sauce.
Cook 1 minute longer. In skillet, bring 1 cup
water to boil. Add mussels and clams, cover, and
steam just until shells open (discard any that
don't open). With slotted spoon, transfer to chili
mixture. Season to taste with salt and pepper.
Serve in bowls with cilantro, jalapeños, cheese,
and limes to add as desired.

Serves 6.

SCALLOPS CHILES RELLENOS

HOW TO ROAST DRIED PEPPERS

Dried peppers should be wiped clean with a damp cloth or paper towels before roasting. Place in a dry skillet over medium-low heat and keep turning until fragrant, 2 to 4 minutes. Be careful not to blacken or the chiles will turn bitter.

8 poblanos, roasted and peeled
2 tablespoons oil
1 onion, diced
2 garlic cloves, minced
2 tomatoes, peeled, seeded, and chopped
1 tablespoon chopped fresh oregano
2 cups fresh corn kernels
1 pound bay scallops
2 cups shredded jack or panela cheese
Coarse salt and freshly ground pepper
2 tablespoons butter
2 tablespoons all-purpose flour
1½ cups milk
⅓ cup grated Parmesan cheese

44

Cut slit in side of each poblano and carefully remove seeds. Set aside.

In large skillet, heat oil. Add onion and cook, stirring frequently, until soft. Add garlic and cook 30 seconds longer. Stir in tomatoes and oregano and bring to boil. Reduce heat and simmer 15 minutes. Stir in corn, scallops, and 1½ cups cheese. Remove from heat and season to taste with salt and pepper.

Preheat oven to 350 degrees F. Stuff chiles with scallop mixture and arrange in single layer in baking dish.

In saucepan, melt butter. Add flour and cook and stir 30 seconds. Gradually stir in milk until smooth. Bring to boil. Stir in remaining ½ cup cheese and cook just until melted. Season to taste with salt and pepper. Pour sauce over poblanos and sprinkle with Parmesan. Bake 20 minutes or until lightly browned on top.

Serves 4 to 6.

See sidebar p.69 for
How to Roast Fresh Peppers.

LINGUINE WITH LOBSTER & PEPPERS

Holland, or Dutch, chiles are a fresh, bright-red chile. They are long, narrow, and thin-skinned, with a hot, sweet flavor. Red jalapeños are a good substitute.

1/2 cup olive oil
6 to 8 Holland reds, stemmed, seeded, and chopped
3 garlic cloves, minced
3 cups cooked lobster, cut into chunks
1 large tomato, peeled, seeded, and chopped
Grated skin of 1 lemon
1/3 cup chopped fresh Italian parsley, basil, or mint
1 pound linguine, cooked and drained
Coarse salt
Lemon wedges

In skillet, heat ¼ cup oil over medium heat. Add chiles and garlic and sauté 1 minute. Stir in lobster and cook 1 minute longer. Add tomato, lemon skin, parsley, and remaining ¼ cup oil and cook just until heated through. Pour over hot cooked linguine, season to taste with salt, and toss thoroughly. Serve with lemon wedges, if desired.

Serves 6.

CHILE'S ROOTS

The original chile plant, classified as a fruit, not a vegetable, hails from either Peru or Bolivia—depending on which anthropologist you ask—circa 7000 B.C. The tiny, pungent red fruit was most widely cultivated in Mexico, where it was deemed important enough to serve as currency as well as food. Seeds were carried by birds throughout Central, South, and southern North America. Modern Mexico still produces the greatest variety of chile peppers, about 140 types at last count.

47

STEAMED MONKFISH WITH SIZZLING CHILE OIL

4 (6-ounce) monkfish fillets
1/4 cup soy sauce
2 tablespoons dry sherry
1/2 cup peanut oil
2 scallions, cut in 2-inch lengths and slivered
2-inch piece of ginger, peeled and thinly slivered
2 teaspoons minced garlic
2 arbols or dried reds, cut in 1/2-inch lengths with seeds
2 teaspoons sesame oil
Salt

Rub 2 tablespoons soy sauce and dry sherry all over fish and place on oil-coated surface for steaming. Assemble remaining ingredients for quick cooking.

Steam fish in wok or steamer 10 to 14 minutes, until opaque in center.

Just before fish is done, warm peanut oil in small saucepan over medium heat about 3 minutes. Stir in scallions, ginger, garlic, arbols, sesame oil, and salt. Cook 30 seconds. Remove from heat and stir in soy sauce.

When fish is done, transfer to serving plates. Drizzle with sizzling oil and serve hot.

Serves 4.

SHRIMP WITH ANCHOS & GARLIC

In this succulent shrimp dish, sweet, smokey dried anchos are used more as a vegetable than a spice.

1 pound large shrimp, shelled and deveined
    Coarse salt and freshly ground pepper
3/4 cup olive oil
10 garlic cloves, thinly sliced
1 to 2 anchos, stemmed, seeded, and
    roughly chopped
1/4 cup lemon or lime juice

Pat shrimp dry and season all over with salt and pepper. Heat oil in large skillet over high heat. Sear shrimp until pink all over, 1 minute per side and transfer to platter.

Reduce heat to medium-low and let pan cool down. Add garlic and anchos. Cook, stirring frequently, until aroma is released, about a minute. Stir in lime juice and seared shrimp, cook an additional minute, tip onto platter, and serve over rice.

Serves 4.

THAI BBQ STEAK

1½ pounds flank steak
  3 tablespoons soy sauce
  4 tablespoons Thai fish sauce
  3 tablespoons lime juice
  2 teaspoons sugar
  1 teaspoon minced fresh ginger
  3 green Thais or serranos, stemmed and chopped
  2 tablespoons minced green onion
  1 tablespoon chopped cilantro

Place steak in shallow dish. Combine 2 tablespoons
soy sauce, 1 tablespoon fish sauce, 1 tablespoon lime
juice, 1 teaspoon sugar, and ginger. Pour over steak.
Marinate at least 1 hour, turning several times.

In blender, combine remaining soy sauce, fish
sauce, lime juice, and sugar. Add chiles. Process until
chiles are finely ground. Transfer to bowl and stir in
green onion and cilantro.

Cook steak over hot coals until done as desired.
Let stand 5 minutes. Slice ½-inch thick on diagonal.
Divide among 4 plates and pour sauce over each.

Serves 4.

JALAPEÑO FLANK STEAK

Beef and peppers are one of those unbeatable combinations. Guaranteed to send a tingle down the spine of your favorite meat-eater.

3 jalapeños
4 garlic cloves, peeled
1/2 tablespoon cracked black pepper
1 tablespoon coarse salt
1/4 cup lime juice
1 tablespoon dried oregano
1/2 cup olive oil
11/2 pounds flank steak

Combine the jalapeños, garlic, black pepper, salt, lime juice, and oregano in a blender or food processor and purée. Pour over steak in shallow roasting pan and rub all over. Cover and marinate in refrigerator 2 to 24 hours. Preheat grill or broiler.

Grill or broil 5 minutes per side for medium-rare. Let sit 5 minutes before slicing. Cut in thin slices across grain and serve hot or cold. Leftovers are great on sandwiches.

Serves 4.

PREDICTING THE HEAT

While the heat of a particular type of chile can vary greatly according to growing conditions (the hotter and dryer the climate, the spicier the chile crop) here are some hints for predicting heat. Small chiles, like serranos and jalapeños, are generally spicier than large ones like Anaheims or New Mexicans. Red varieties are riper or sweeter than green. Dried chiles are often more flavorful but less hot than their fresh counterparts. (But don't let pequins or arbols fool you. They are definitely hot.)

53

CHILE VERDE

2 tablespoons oil
2 pounds boneless pork, cut into 1-inch cubes
1 large onion, chopped
10 to 12 Anaheims, roasted, peeled, and chopped
3 garlic cloves, chopped
1 teaspoon dried oregano
1/2 teaspoon each ground coriander and cumin
2 (18-ounce) cans tomatillos, drained and chopped
1 (14 1/2-ounce) can chicken broth
Coarse salt and freshly ground pepper
Sour cream (optional)
Thinly sliced jalapeños (optional)

In large pot, heat oil over medium-high heat.

Add meat and cook, stirring frequently, until browned on all sides. Add onion and cook, stirring frequently, until translucent. Stir in Anaheims, garlic, oregano, coriander, and cumin. Cook and stir 2 minutes longer.

Add tomatillos and chicken broth and bring to boil. Reduce heat, cover and simmer, stirring occasionally 45 minutes to 1 hour, or until meat is tender. Season to taste with salt and pepper. Serve with sour cream and jalapeños, if desired.

Serves 6 to 8.

The same chile may go by different names in different places—the fresh poblano, for instance, is called a pasilla in parts of California and poblano elsewhere. A good general rule to follow is to shop more by appearance than by name. If your market doesn't seem to carry poblanos, purchase a medium, wide-shouldered dark-green chile instead. Chances are it will be similar to a poblano.

CARIBBEAN PORK SOUSE

This traditional dish comes from Christiana Wise, from the island of Montserrat in the Caribbean.

3 pounds pork shoulder or butt
  Salt and black pepper
2 onions
3 tablespoons vegetable oil
9 cups water
1 bay leaf
4 garlic cloves, minced
2 to 4 serranos, thinly sliced with seeds
6 whole cloves
1/2 cup lemon juice

Preheat oven to 350 degrees F.

Trim meat of excess fat and season all over with salt and pepper. Peel onions, then quarter one and thinly slice the other.

Heat oil in large, heavy dutch oven over high heat. Sear meat until brown all over. Pour in 7 cups water, quartered onion and bay leaf. Bring nearly to boil. Cover and transfer to oven. Bake until tender, 1½ hours. Remove meat to platter to cool.

Meanwhile prepare seasonings. In large ceramic or glass bowl, place sliced onion, garlic, serranos, cloves, lemon juice, and about 2 teaspoons salt. Bring 2 cups water to a boil and pour over seasonings. Stir to combine.

Cut meat across grain into thin slices and add to souse mixture. Stir to combine. Cover with plastic wrap and let sit, at room temperature, 4 hours or refrigerate as long as a day. Serve room temperature with rice or bread.

Serves 4.

KUNG PAU CHICKEN

Serve this Chinese restaurant standard with plenty of white rice.

- 3/4 pound skinless, boneless chicken breast
- 1 tablespoon dry sherry
- 2 teaspoons soy sauce
- 1 tablespoon cornstarch
- 1/2 cup plus 1 tablespoon peanut or corn oil
- 1 cup raw peanuts
- 1 tablespoon minced fresh ginger
- 1 tablespoon minced garlic
- 3 to 6 dried red chiles or arbols, roughly chopped with seeds
- 1 bell pepper, seeded and cut in 1/2-inch cubes
- 3 scallions, cut in 1/2-inch slices

Sauce:

- 2 tablespoons soy sauce
- 2 tablespoons dry sherry
- 1 teaspoon sesame oil
- 1/2 teaspoon sugar
- 1/2 teaspoon Chinese chile sauce

Cut chicken into ½-inch cubes. Place in bowl with sherry, soy, and cornstarch. Toss well to evenly coat and refrigerate.

Heat ½ cup of oil in wok over high heat. Fry peanuts, stirring frequently, just until golden and then drain on paper towels. Carefully pour off all but 2 tablespoons oil from wok.

Stir-fry chicken just until white. Transfer to platter with slotted spoon.

Add remaining tablespoon of oil to wok over high heat. Stir-fry ginger, garlic, and red chiles less than a minute. Add bell pepper and scallions and fry about 20 seconds longer. Pour in the sauce ingredients, chicken, and peanuts. Stir and toss until well combined. Serve hot.

Serves 4.

PORK PICADILLO CHILES RELLENOS

Picadillo is a typical sweet-and-sour Mexican stuffing for peppers. Look for big, wide, firm poblanos for stuffing.

8 poblanos
3 tablespoons vegetable oil
1 medium onion, diced
1 garlic clove, minced
1 pound ground pork
6 canned plum tomatoes, seeded and diced
1/4 cup raisins
2 tablespoons red wine vinegar
1/4 teaspoon each ground cumin and cinnamon
   Salt and black pepper
1/2 cup flour
2 eggs, beaten
   Sour cream for garnish

Roast and peel chiles, being careful not to cook through flesh. Carefully cut one lengthwise slit in each and remove seed sac beneath stem. Set aside for stuffing.

Heat 1 tablespoon oil in large skillet over medium heat. Sauté onion and garlic until soft, about 5 minutes. Add pork and cook, stirring and tossing, until evenly browned. Add remaining ingredients and reduce heat. Cook over medium-low heat, stirring occasionally, until liquid is evaporated, about 1/2 hour.

Divide pork mixture and stuff into each chile. Dip each first in flour and then in egg to lightly coat.

Heat remaining oil in large skillet over medium heat. Sauté chiles, split side up, until lightly browned on 3 sides, 2 minutes total. Serve with dollops of sour cream.

Serves 4.

PASTA BRAVA CON JALAPEÑO

3 tablespoons olive oil
2 garlic cloves, minced
4 jalapeños, stemmed, seeded, and minced
1½ pounds plum tomatoes, peeled, seeded,
    and coarsely chopped
  Coarse salt
1 pound penne, cooked and drained
3 tablespoons chopped cilantro
½ cup crumbled cotija or feta cheese

In large skillet, heat oil over medium heat. Add garlic and jalapeños and sauté 1 minute. Add tomatoes and cook, stirring occasionally, about 10 minutes. Season to taste with salt. Pour over hot penne in bowl and add cilantro. Toss to combine. Serve sprinkled with cheese.

Serves 4 to 6.

POLENTA ARRABBIATA WITH POACHED EGGS

2 tablespoons olive oil
2 garlic cloves, minced
3 Holland reds
1 (28-ounce) can chopped tomatoes
2 tablespoons chopped Italian parsley
  Coarse salt and freshly ground pepper
1 cup uncooked polenta
8 eggs, poached
  Freshly grated Parmesan cheese

In skillet, heat oil over medium heat. Add garlic and chiles and sauté 30 seconds. Add tomatoes and bring to boil. Reduce heat and simmer 10 minutes. Stir in parsley and simmer 5 minutes longer. Season to taste with salt and pepper.

Meanwhile, cook polenta according to package directions. Poach eggs.

To serve, divide polenta into 4 shallow bowls and top each with 2 eggs. Spoon sauce on top and sprinkle with Parmesan.

Serves 4.

BEANLESS BREAKFAST BURRITOS

Scrambled eggs with roasted peppers wrapped in a warm flour tortilla—not a bad way to start the day or end it.

2 flour tortillas
4 eggs
¼ cup heavy cream
Salt
2 teaspoons butter
2 poblanos, roasted, peeled, seeded and diced
¼ cup sour cream
Chopped red onion, jalapeño, cilantro, and tomatoes for garnish

Wrap tortillas in foil and warm in 350 degree F. oven 10 minutes.

Lightly beat eggs with cream and salt. Melt butter in medium skillet over medium heat. Pour in eggs and then diced poblanos. Reduce heat and stir constantly until small soft curds form. Remove from heat.

Place each tortilla on a plate. Spread with sour cream. Spoon eggs in center. Top with onion, jalapeños, cilantro, and tomatoes. Fold to enclose, and serve.

Serves 2.

IF YOU CAN'T TAKE THE HEAT...

Use fewer peppers, or omit the seeds entirely. You will still get a pleasant chile buzz. In emergencies, you can douse the flames with tortillas, rice, beans, milk or milk products, salt and/or sugar. Water and beer are not as good since they spread the chile oils around.

CONTENTS

HOT
SALSAS

SALSA FRESCA

3 large ripe tomatoes
1/2 red onion, diced
1 to 2 serranos, finely diced with seeds
1 bunch chopped fresh cilantro
Juice of 1 lime
Salt
Tabasco to taste

Core tomatoes and finely chop. Place in mixing bowl and combine with remaining ingredients, seasoning to taste with salt and Tabasco. Salsa Fresca tastes best served within 3 or 4 hours. Keep refrigerated until serving time. Great with meat, poultry, fish, cheese, and chips.

Makes 4 cups.

ROASTED PEPPER SALSA

- 3 poblanos, roasted, peeled, seeded, and julienned
- 3 red bells, roasted, peeled, seeded, and julienned
- 2 garlic cloves, roasted, peeled, and thinly sliced
- 1/2 red onion, thinly sliced
- 3 tablespoons lemon or lime juice
- 6 tablespoons olive oil
  Salt and black pepper
- 2 tablespoons chopped fresh oregano

Mix ingredients together in large bowl. Serve at once with grilled or sautéed fish or reserve up to 6 hours. Serve room temperature.

Serves 4.

HOW TO ROAST FRESH PEPPERS

Fresh peppers can be roasted directly on a gas burner or under the broiler. Cook until charred all over and then transfer to a plastic bag to sweat. Seal the bag and let steam 10 minutes or longer. Remove blackened skins with fingertips or carefully scrape with a paring knife. Do not place under running water to peel or you will lose flavor as the oils wash off.

See p. 44 for How to Roast Dried Peppers.

CHILE ARBOL SALSA

½ pound tomatoes
½ pound tomatillos, peeled
½ cup arbols
1 medium onion, chopped
2 garlic cloves, peeled and crushed
2 cups water
Salt and black pepper

Preheat broiler. Place tomatoes and tomatillos on baking tray and broil, turning frequently, until evenly charred. Transfer to saucepan with remaining ingredients.

Bring to boil, reduce to simmer, and cook about 20 minutes. Transfer to food processor or blender and purée. Strain, if desired, and serve chilled with grilled beef, lamb, or pork.

Makes 2 cups.

PAPAYA SALSA

1 large ripe papaya, peeled, seeded, and diced
3 jalapeños, stemmed, seeded and minced
¼ cup minced red onion
¼ cup chopped cilantro
2 tablespoons lime juice
½ teaspoon grated lime rind

Combine all ingredients in bowl. Toss thoroughly.
Serve with grilled chicken, fish, or sausages.

Makes about 1½ cups.

*Arbols or chiles de arbols, also
known as dried red chiles, are
the papery thin, long, dry red
chiles sold by the bag in the
supermarket and used extensively
in Chinese and Mexican cooking.
They are extremely hot and get
even hotter as they cook.*

CHIPOTLE SALSA

 4 canned chipotles, minced
 2 large tomatoes, diced
 1/2 small onion, diced
 1/4 cup chopped cilantro
    Juice of 1 lime
    Coarse salt

In bowl, combine all ingredients. Stir to
blend. Season to taste with salt. Serve over
grilled fish, seafood, or chicken or with chips.

Makes about 2 cups.

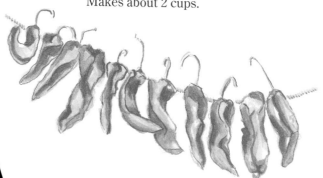

SMOOTH JALAPEÑO SALSA

  1 tablespoon vegetable oil
  1/2 medium onion, chopped
  2 garlic cloves, crushed
  1 medium tomato, peeled and chopped
  1/2 teaspoon salt
  4 to 6 jalapeños, stemmed, seeded,
    and chopped

In skillet, heat oil over medium heat.
Add onion and sauté until soft. Add garlic
and cook 30 seconds then stir in tomato and
salt. Simmer 5 minutes. Transfer to blender
and add jalapeños. Process until puréed.
Serve room temperature or chilled with
lightly sautéed vegetables or chips.

Makes about 1 cup.

TOMATILLO SALSA DE ARBOL

2 teaspoons vegetable oil
6 arbols, stemmed and crumbled
4 garlic cloves, peeled and crushed
⅓ cup diced onion
2 (18-ounce) cans tomatillos, drained and coarsely chopped
Coarse salt

In skillet, heat oil over medium-high.

Add arbols and garlic and cook, stirring occasionally, 1 to 2 minutes. Transfer mixture to blender or food processor and add onion and tomatillos. Process to blend.

Season to taste with salt. Serve with grilled steak, chicken, or chips.

Makes about 2 cups.

HANDLING THE HEAT

Chiles' legendary heat is produced in the placenta—the sack under the stem—and carried in the seeds and veins. If you want less heat and more flavor simply remove seeds and veins and just use the fruit, or if you want to turn the thermostat up, chop the seeds to release more oil (or capsaicin). Some cooks protect their hands with gloves when handling chiles. If you choose not to, make sure you wash hands, knives, and cutting boards with soap and water and be careful not to rub your eyes after handling chiles. Capsaicin spreads like wildfire.

The ancient Aztecs had a scale for rating chiles that ranged from hot to very, very hot to runaway hot. The modern equivalent is the Scoville unit, an objective measuring system developed by pharmacologist Wilbur Scoville that isolates and measures the amount of capsaicin or pungent oil in chile peppers.

CONTENTS

SLIGHTLY INSANE SIDE DISHES

THAI FRIED RICE

The key to restaurant-quality fried rice is to begin with cold rice. With its red and green peppers, this is a pretty side dish.

Serranos are a small, slim, fresh green or red chile (about 2 inches long), similar in appearance to jalapeños but about twice as hot. Delicious in salsas and salads and a good substitute for Thai peppers. Use 2 serranos to each Thai.

4 tablespoons vegetable oil
2 lop cheung or Chinese sausages, thinly sliced
1/2 pound medium shrimp, peeled, deveined, and patted dry
2 eggs, beaten
2 serranos, seeded and diced
1 garlic clove, minced
3 scallions, thinly sliced
3 cups cold cooked rice
  Thai fish sauce
2 Thai red chiles, seeded and diced

Heat 2 tablespoons of oil in wok over high heat.

Stir-fry sausages until edges are crisp. Transfer to platter with slotted spoon. Stir-fry shrimp just until pink and transfer to platter. Drain liquid from wok, leaving about a spoonful of oil. Pour in eggs, swirling to make a thin, puffy layer. Quickly scramble into bite-sized pieces and transfer to platter.

Return wok to high heat and swirl in remaining oil. Stir-fry serranos, garlic, and scallions less than a minute. Add rice, stirring and tossing to evenly coat and fry. Return sausage, shrimp, and egg to wok, drizzle in fish sauce to taste, and stir and toss less than a minute. Turn out onto platter and garnish with red chiles.

Serves 4.

CITRUS CHILE RICE

2 tablespoons butter
½ cup diced onion
⅓ cup lightly crushed vermicelli
1 cup long-grain rice
2 Holland reds, stemmed, seeded, and chopped
Juice and grated rind of 1 orange
1 (14½-ounce) can chicken or vegetable broth
Coarse salt and freshly ground pepper
Chopped cilantro

In medium saucepan, melt butter over medium-high heat.

Add onion and cook just until translucent. Add vermicelli and cook, stirring frequently, until golden. Add rice and stir to coat. Add chiles, orange juice and rind, and broth and bring to boil. Stir again, reduce heat, cover and simmer 20 minutes. Remove from heat and let stand 5 minutes. Season to taste with salt and pepper, fluffing with fork. Serve sprinkled with cilantro.

Serves 4.

SAUTÉED ZUCCHINI, CORN & CHILES

2 tablespoons vegetable oil
1 small onion, sliced
2 garlic cloves, minced
4 Anaheims, roasted, peeled, stemmed, seeded, and thinly sliced
1½ pounds zucchini, trimmed, and sliced ½-inch thick
1 tomato, peeled and chopped
½ cup chicken or vegetable broth
½ cup corn kernels
Coarse salt and freshly ground pepper
1 cup shredded jack or panela cheese

In skillet, heat oil.

Add onion and sauté until soft. Stir in garlic and Anaheims. Sauté 30 seconds longer. Stir in zucchini and tomato and cook 1 to 2 minutes. Add broth, cover, and simmer 5 minutes. Stir in corn and simmer 5 minutes longer. Season to taste with salt and pepper. Stir in cheese and cook just until cheese begins to melt. Serve immediately.

Serves 6.

🌶🌶🌶

SPICY COLD EGGPLANT

1 pound Japanese eggplant, sliced ½-inch thick
2 teaspoons dried red pepper flakes
1 tablespoon oil
3 tablespoons soy sauce
2 tablespoons rice vinegar
2 teaspoons sugar
1 teaspoon sesame oil
1 green onion, thinly sliced on diagonal

Place eggplant slices in steamer and cook over simmering water until soft, about 15 minutes. Set aside.

In small skillet, heat oil. Add hot pepper flakes and cook 30 seconds. Remove from heat and stir in soy sauce, vinegar, sugar, and sesame oil. Pour over eggplant. Chill. Sprinkle with green onion and serve.

Serves 4.

COWBOY BEANS

1 pound dried pinto beans
4 thick bacon slices, coarsely chopped
1 onion, chopped
3 garlic cloves, chopped
8 to 10 Anaheims, roasted, peeled, seeded,
   and thinly sliced
1 (28-ounce) can whole tomatoes, cut up
   Coarse salt and freshly ground pepper

Soak beans in water to cover at least 8 hours or overnight.

In large pot, cook bacon over medium-high heat until browned. Add onion and cook until translucent. Add garlic and chiles and cook 1 minute longer.

Drain beans, rinse, and add to pot along with tomatoes and enough water to cover. Bring to boil, reduce heat, cover partially, and cook 1 hour, stirring occasionally. Uncover and simmer, stirring occasionally, until beans are tender, about 1 to 2 hours or longer. Season to taste with salt and pepper.

Serves 8 to 10.

🌶🌶🌶
RAJAS CON CREMA

Rajas are roasted pepper strips coated with cream. They are traditionally served as an accompaniment to carne asada and are quite delicious all on their own with warm tortillas for tucking into.

2 tablespoons olive oil
1 medium onion, thinly sliced
3 garlic cloves, peeled and slivered
  Salt
6 large poblanos, roasted, seeded, and
  thinly sliced
1/2 cup heavy cream
1 teaspoon dried oregano
  Juice of 1 lime
1/4 cup crumbled feta cheese

Heat oil in medium skillet over medium heat.

Sauté onion and garlic with salt until garlic is golden, about 6 minutes. Add poblanos, reduce heat to low, and sauté 2 minutes longer.

Pour in cream and oregano. Cook over medium heat until cream is thick enough to coat vegetables. Sprinkle with lime juice and cheese, stir, and remove from heat. Serve hot.

Serves 4 to 6.

MEXICO'S PEPPER MADNESS

No other country's ardor can compare with Mexico's passion for peppers. Unlike the cuisines of India, Thailand, China, Korea, some African nations, and the Caribbean, which employ the same few chiles (mainly as a spice to add heat), Mexican cooks use about 140 varieties as a vegetable as well as a spice to add several shades of flavor as well as heat to their cooking.

ANCHO CORN CAKES

Store fresh chiles in the vegetable bin of the refrigerator, where they will keep a week or longer. When they turn soft, wrinkled, or brown, they are no longer good. Dried chiles are best stored in plastic bags in the freezer, where they keep indefinitely without attracting bugs. Just let them sit a minute or two at room temperature to soften before using.

86

2 to 4 anchos
1/2 cup all-purpose flour
1/2 cup yellow cornmeal
1/2 teaspoon baking powder
3/4 teaspoon salt
1/2 teaspoon crushed dry oregano
3/4 cup milk
1/4 cup melted butter
1 egg
1 cup corn kernels
 Oil
 Sour cream
 Tomatillo Salsa de Arbol (see p.74)

Place anchos in small saucepan and cover with water. Bring to boil, remove from heat, cover, and let stand 10 minutes. Drain. When cool enough to handle, remove skin, stems, and seeds, then finely dice. Set aside.

In bowl, combine flour, cornmeal, baking powder, salt, and oregano. In separate bowl, mix milk with melted butter and egg. Stir into flour mixture. Fold in corn and anchos.

Ladle batter onto hot, lightly oiled griddle to make 3-inch cakes. Cook over medium-high heat 2 minutes per side or until golden. Transfer to plate and keep warm. Repeat with remaining batter. Serve warm with sour cream and Tomatillo Salsa de Arbol.

Serves 4.

Anchos, the dried version of poblanos, are the most popular dried chile. They are a brown, wrinkled, wide-shouldered chile with a distinctive sweet, fruity, peppery flavor and mild heat. They are typically puréed as a base for sauces and moles or thinly sliced and added to sauces as a final bit of chewy texture and smokey flavor at the end.

CHEESE CHIPOTLE SOUFFLÉ

3 tablespoons butter
3 tablespoons all-purpose flour
1 cup milk
1 cup shredded jack or panela cheese
3 canned chipotles, minced
3/4 teaspoon salt
3 eggs, separated
Salsa Fresca (see p.68)

In saucepan, melt butter over medium heat. Stir in flour, then gradually stir in milk. Cook, stirring constantly, until thickened. Add cheese, chipotles, and salt and stir until cheese melts.

In small bowl, lightly beat yolks. Stir some hot cheese mixture into yolks then return to pan and stir to blend. Cook and stir over low heat 1 minute longer. Remove from heat, place plastic wrap over surface, and cool to room temperature.

Preheat oven to 350 degrees F. In large bowl, beat egg whites until stiff but not dry. Lightly stir about 1/4 cup whites into cheese mixture, then fold in remaining whites. Spoon into 5- to 6-cup buttered soufflé dish and bake 35 to 40 minutes or until puffed and browned. Serve immediately. Pass Salsa Fresca at table, if desired.

Serves 4.

CONTENTS

SURPRISE
ENDINGS

CHOCOLATE PEPPER COOKIES

We took a little license here with black pepper rather than chile—the two peppers are not related—and came up with one diabolical chocolate cookie. This is an adaptation of Los Angeles chefs Mary Sue Milliken's and Susan Feniger's terrific scooter cookie.

1/2 cup currants
2 tablespoons Kahlua
2 ounces unsweetened chocolate
4 ounces bittersweet chocolate
3 tablespoons butter
6 tablespoons flour
1/4 teaspoon baking powder
1/4 teaspoon salt
1/4 teaspoon cinnamon
1/2 to 1 teaspoon cracked black pepper
2 eggs
3/4 cup sugar
1 teaspoon vanilla
2/3 cup chocolate chips

Preheat oven to 350 degrees F.

Line cookie sheets with parchment paper.
Combine currants with Kahlua in small saucepan
and warm over low heat. Set aside to cool.

Combine unsweetened and bittersweet
chocolates with butter in heavy saucepan and melt,
stirring frequently, over low heat. Set aside to cool.

In small bowl, stir together flour, baking powder,
salt, cinnamon, and cracked pepper.

Beat eggs and sugar until pale and thick,
5 minutes. Beat in vanilla. Pour melted chocolate
into beaten egg mixture and fold to combine. Fold
in flour mixture. Gently stir in currants and chocolate
chips. (The dough should be loose.)

Drop by spoonfuls onto lined cookie sheets.
Bake 8 to 10 minutes, until tops are cracked and
shiny and cookies are slightly puffy. Let cool
5 minutes on sheets and then transfer to racks.

Makes about 20 cookies.

🌶🌶🌶
SANGRITA ICE

These refreshing citrus spice ices make a nice between course palate-tingler or dessert.

> 2 cups chopped tomatoes
> 3 jalapeños, stemmed, seeded, and chopped
> Juice of 2 oranges
> Juice of 3 limes
> 1/3 cup tequila
> 1/4 cup sugar
> Lime wedges and jalapeño slices

In food processor, purée tomatoes and jalapeños until smooth. Add orange and lime juices, tequila, and sugar. Process to mix. Pour into ice cube trays and freeze.

At serving time, place about 6 cubes into food processor and process with pulses to break into chunks. Then process continuously until slushy. Spoon into serving dishes and garnish with lime wedges and jalapeño slices. Repeat with remaining cubes.

Serves about 6.

JALAPEÑO LEMONADE

Consider yourself warned. If this sweet, tart, wet, and wild cooler sits past 3 hours we are not responsible for the damages. It will get powerfully hot.

- 1/2 cup sugar
- 6 1/2 cups water
- 3/4 cup fresh lemon juice
- 2 jalapeños, stemmed and sliced with seeds

Combine sugar and 1/2 cup water in small saucepan. Simmer until sugar dissolves and liquid is clear, about 3 minutes.

Combine in pitcher with remaining water, lemon juice, and sliced jalapeños. Stir and refrigerate 1 to 3 hours. Strain or serve with jalapeños, depending on pain threshold.

Makes enough for 6 tall glasses.

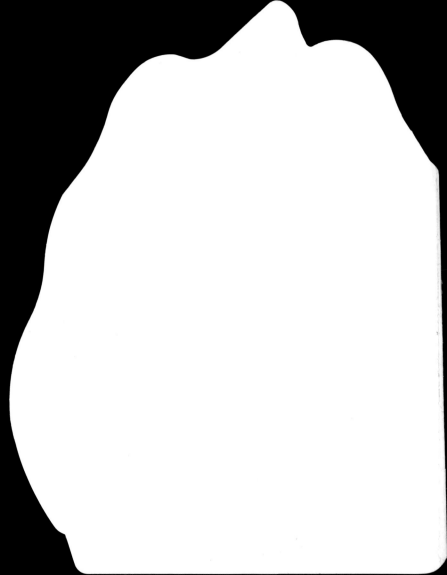